UNDERSTANDING
WHO YOU ARE
IN *SEEING YOURSELF AS GOD SEES YOU*
CHRIST

Study Guide

KENNETH COPELAND

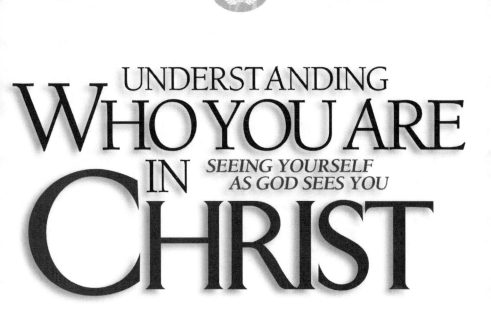

UNDERSTANDING
WHO YOU ARE
IN
SEEING YOURSELF AS GOD SEES YOU
CHRIST

Study Guide

KENNETH COPELAND

KENNETH
COPELAND
PUBLICATIONS

Unless otherwise noted, all Scripture quotations are taken from the *King James Version* of the Bible.

Scripture quotations marked *The Amplified Bible,* Old Testament © 1965, 1987 by the Zondervan Corporation. The Amplified New Testament © 1958, 1987 by The Lockman Foundation. Used by permission.

Understanding Who You Are in Christ Study Guide
Previously published as *Reality of Redemption*

ISBN 10-1-57562-644-0   30-0720
ISBN 13-978-1-57562-664-2

19 18 17 16 15 14   11 10 9 8 7 6

Kenneth Copeland Publications
Fort Worth, Texas 76192-0001

For more information about Kenneth Copeland Ministries, visit kcm.org or call 1-800-600-7395 (U.S. only) or +1-817-852-6000.

"Now to him that is of power to stablish you according to my gospel, and the preaching of Jesus Christ, according to the revelation of the mystery, which was kept secret since the world began, But now is made manifest, and by the scriptures of the prophets, according to the commandment of the everlasting God, made known to all nations for the obedience of faith."

Romans 16:25-26

The plan of redemption has been unveiled
through the Word of God.

CD ONE
Reality of Redemption

A Study of the Steps to the Highest Kind of Faith Is a Study of the Plan of Redemption

*T*he plan of redemption has been unveiled through the Word of God. The reality of redemption is not an idea or a psychological fact. It is a spiritual fact.

Your Faith Will Be Strengthened According to Your Revelation of the Plan of Redemption

FOCUS: "Now to Him Who is able to strengthen you in the faith which is in accordance with my Gospel and the preaching of (concerning) Jesus Christ (the Messiah), according to the revelation (the unveiling) of the mystery of the plan of redemption which was kept in silence and secret for long ages" (Romans 16:25, *The Amplified Bible*).

The believer is faced with the responsibility of living out from under the curse in a dying world. An understanding of the plan of redemption is the key, so let's look at what happened.

First of all, Adam's high treason resulted in spiritual death for all mankind. He was brought under the dominion of Satan.

That's why there had to be an incarnation. A man who was not under the lordship of Satan had to come into the world. It had to be a birth without the corruption of a man. There had to be a man who would take back the dominion that Adam lost.

God spoke and outlined the plan of redemption after Satan beguiled Eve and Adam committed high treason. The plan has now been revealed through the Word (Romans 16:26). The Bible was written to show that plan and the authority believers have now. That's why Satan fights the Word.

> *Your faith will operate on the level of your knowledge of the plan of redemption.*

Jesus was the last Adam, an eternal man. He made Himself obedient to death, putting Himself in the hands of His enemy, Satan.

Jesus went to hell to pay the price for Adam's high treason. When God raised Him from the dead, He became untouchable by death. He became the firstborn of many brethren (see Romans 8:29). What the believer receives from God depends on the amount of knowledge he has concerning the plan of redemption. That's because your faith will operate on the level of your knowledge of the plan of redemption. *(Phil 1:8)*

Second Peter 1:2-4 says the believer can escape the corruption that is in the world, partake of the divine nature of God, and have grace and peace multiplied unto himself, because God's divine power has already provided everything that pertains to life and godliness.

God likeness

The Believer *Has Been* Redeemed

FOCUS: Colossians 1:12-14 says, "Giving thanks unto the Father, which **hath** made us meet to be partakers of the inheritance of the saints in light; Who **hath** delivered us from the power of darkness, and **hath** translated us into the kingdom of his dear Son: In whom we **have redemption** through his blood, even the forgiveness of sins." The believer is holy and unblameable in the sight of God (Colossians 1:22).

The Body of Christ is as free from the dominion of Satan as Jesus was when God raised Him from the dead. Satan no longer has authority over the believer who has a working revelation of redemption.

As believers, we have been taken out of the dominion of Satan and placed in the kingdom of God's dear Son. We are as free from Satan as Adam was before he sinned. As we submit ourselves to God and resist the devil, he will flee. He has no right over the believer. He recognizes the authority we have and the ability we possess to enforce it.

Key　　The moment the believer takes his place as a child of God, he can begin to partake of his inheritance. Philippians 2:5-6 says, "Let this mind be in you, which was also in Christ Jesus: Who, being in the form of God, thought it not robbery to be equal with God." It is not robbery to be called a joint heir with Jesus. Ephesians 2:1, 6 says, "And you [He made alive], when you were dead (slain) by [your] trespasses and sins…And He raised us up together with Him and made us sit down together [giving us joint seating with Him] in the heavenly sphere [by virtue of our being] in Christ Jesus…" *(The Amplified Bible).* The believer is not only a joint heir with Christ Jesus, but he is an heir of God—entitled to the blessings of his inheritance.

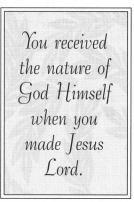

You received the nature of God Himself when you made Jesus Lord.

But the believer can only believe for the parts of the plan of redemption that he knows about. If all he knows about is salvation, that's all he can receive. But when he learns about the other benefits of redemption such as healing, he can begin to use his faith for those as well. ✍

The power that God wrought in Christ when He raised Him from the dead is the same power that works in the believer today. The nature of God Himself has been imparted to his spirit as a new creation.

Now Begin Enjoying It

Now it is the responsibility of the believer to walk in the light of the redemptive work that was wrought for him in Christ. The Apostle Paul said, "Be not conformed to this world: but be ye transformed by the renewing of your mind, that ye may prove what is that good, and acceptable, and perfect, will of God" (Romans 12:2). It's time to renew your mind and take control of your body, making it live in relation to what's already happened to your heart. Let redemption become a reality in your life.

CD 1 Outlined

I. Knowledge of redemption
   A. The plan has been revealed through the Scriptures
      (Romans 16:26)
   B. The redemption plan was spoken after the
      Fall of Man

II. Jesus became a man
   A. Not born under Satan's rulership
   B. Obedient to death
   C. Untouchable by death
   D. Firstborn from the dead

III. The believer is reconciled to God through the
   redemptive work of Christ, His death in His body
   of flesh (Colossians 1:22)
   A. Holy
   B. Unblameable
   C. Unreproveable

IV. The power of God is at work in the believer today
   A. It's the same power God wrought in Christ when He
      raised Him from the dead
   B. The nature of God was imparted to the believer at
      the new birth

V. The believer is responsible to walk in the light of the
   redemptive work of Christ
   A. Don't be conformed to the world
   B. Renew your mind

Study Questions

(1) List the benefits of the revelation of redemption. _____

_____

_____

_____

(2) What would knowledge do for those of "like and precious faith" (2 Peter 1:2-4)? _____

_____

_____

_____

(3) How does the believer look in the sight of God? _____

_____

_____

_____

(4) When can the believer operate in his inheritance as a child of God? _____

_____

_____

(5) When did Jesus become untouchable by death? _____

_____

_____

_____

Study Notes

"Grace and peace be multiplied unto you through the knowledge of God, and of Jesus our Lord...."
2 Peter 1:2

2

"*For he hath made him to be sin for us, who knew no sin; that we might be made the righteousness of God in him.*"

2 Corinthians 5:21

Jesus was our substitute. He became what we were so we could become what He is now.

CD TWO
Substitution and Identification

There Are Two Families in the Earth. As Believers, We No Longer Identify With Satan and His Family—Now We Identify With Jesus and the Family of God!

The pivot point around which Christianity revolves is substitution and identification. When the believer identifies with the family of God, he learns about his authority.

Jesus Was Your Substitute— You Were Crucified With Him at Calvary and Resurrected With Him

✎ FOCUS: "I am crucified with Christ: nevertheless I live; yet not I, but Christ liveth in me: and the life which I now live in the flesh I live by the faith of the Son of God, who loved me, and gave himself for me" (Galatians 2:20).

Second Corinthians 5:21 states that Jesus became sin so we could become righteous. He became what we were so we could become what He is now.

The greatness of God's power to us who believe is the same power that was used in Christ when He raised Him from the dead (see Ephesians 1-2). Jesus was raised a *new creature.* He was the first of a new race of men that became the family of God. He was manifested in the flesh and justified in the spirit. The Spirit of God quickened Jesus' dead spirit and made it alive after the claims of justice were satisfied.

Jesus then became the firstborn of many brethren.

> *A born-again man defeated Satan. The believer is the very image of that man.*

He was declared to be the Son of God when He was raised from the dead. Acts 13:33 says, "…Thou art my Son, this day have I begotten thee." And Romans 1:4 in *The Amplified Bible* says, "And [as to His divine nature] according to the Spirit of holiness was openly designated the Son of God…by His resurrection from the dead, even Jesus Christ our Lord...."

A born-again man defeated Satan. The believer is the very image of that man. The same power used to raise Jesus from the dead, raised the believer from death, trespasses and sin. Judgment was passed on Satan. God could re-create a new race of mankind in His likeness.

As new creations in Christ, we are no longer children of disobedience as outlined in Ephesians 2. We have made Jesus our Lord. We have walked out of the family of Satan and into the family of God. ◆

God No Longer Sees You Under the Curse, Unworthy, Sick or Poor

✎ **FOCUS:** "Christ hath redeemed us from the curse of the law, being made a curse for us: for it is written, Cursed is every one that hangeth on a tree" (Galatians 3:13).

> *Since God sees us redeemed from the curse, we should see ourselves this way too!*

Since God sees us redeemed from the curse, likewise we too should see ourselves this way. We have been delivered from the power of darkness and the authority of Satan.

We have been translated into the kingdom of God's dear Son (Colossians 1:13-15). We should now identify with the family of God in our actions and speech.

If you're talking fear, doubt and unbelief, you're identifying with Adam. Instead, identify with Jesus. Get your mind in line with the Word of God. Start talking it, acting it, living it.

The substitution becomes the believer's identification. Jesus died— that's the substitution— so I could be alive—that's the identification. Jesus defeated Satan; the believer identifies with the victory. He went to hell as the substitute, in order to take the believer to heaven. He was cast out of the presence of God for believers to be welcome there.

Now Begin Enjoying It

Allow your identification with Jesus as your substitute to be a living reality in your life. Romans 5:17 says, "For if by one man's offence death reigned by one; much more they which receive abundance of grace and of the gift of righteousness shall reign in life by one, Jesus Christ."

CD 2 Outlined

I. Jesus was the substitute for mankind
  A. We were crucified with Him
    1. He became as mankind
    2. He became sin
  B. We were resurrected with Him
    1. He was justified and declared righteous
    2. Mankind was justified and declared righteous

II. Resurrection power
  A. Jesus was raised from the dead
    1. Jesus was the first of a new race
    2. Satan was defeated by a born-again man
  B. The believer is raised by the same power
    1. A new creature
      a. In His image
      b. A new family
    2. Given authority over Satan
      a. Because of Jesus' victory

III. Jesus' substitution—the believer's identification
  A. He became a curse—the believer receives blessings
  B. His death produced the believer's new life
  C. He entered hell—the believer enters heaven

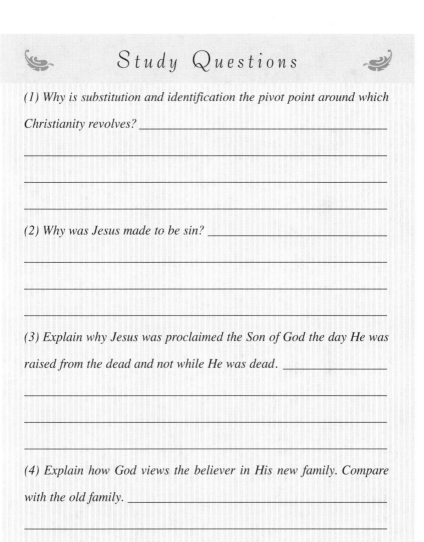

Study Questions

(1) Why is substitution and identification the pivot point around which Christianity revolves? _____

_____

_____

_____

(2) Why was Jesus made to be sin? _____

_____

_____

_____

(3) Explain why Jesus was proclaimed the Son of God the day He was raised from the dead and not while He was dead. _____

_____

_____

_____

(4) Explain how God views the believer in His new family. Compare with the old family. _____

_____

_____

(5) What is the importance of knowing Jesus as the substitute? _____

_____

_____

_____

Study Notes

"But God, who is rich in mercy,
for his great love wherewith he loved us."
Ephesians 2:4

"And when Abram was ninety years old and nine, the Lord appeared to Abram, and said unto him, I am the Almighty God; walk before me, and be thou perfect. And I will make my covenant between me and thee...."

Genesis 17:1-2

God originated the blood covenant with a man called Abram.

CD THREE
The Blood Covenant-Making God

God's Covenant With Abram
Opened the Door for Jesus to
Come Into the Earth…It Paved
the Way for the Ultimate
Covenant That Would Change
Everything

An Understanding of Covenant Will Give You the Ability to Receive What Belongs to You as a Believer

FOCUS: "And when Abram was ninety years old and nine, the Lord appeared to Abram, and said unto him, I am the Almighty God; walk before me, and be thou perfect. And I will make my covenant between me and thee, and will multiply thee exceedingly. And Abram fell on his face: and God talked with him, saying, As for me, behold, my covenant is with thee…" (Genesis 17:1-4).

In Genesis 17, God introduced Himself to Abraham as the "Almighty God." The Hebrew translation of this is El Shaddai, the Supreme Provider of all things.

At that time, no man on earth knew God. Adam had committed high treason and gave his authority to Satan. As a result, God was on the outside looking in. He had no legal grounds to deal with any human being on earth because they belonged to Satan.

> *The covenant agreement with Abraham allowed God to operate in the earth.*

God needed a contract or agreement with a man by which He could legally bring forth the redemption plan that could set man free.

God personally made a covenant with Abraham. If Abraham would follow the covenant, as outlined by God, it would be counted unto him as righteousness.

In Genesis 17:4, the word covenant means "a blood flow" or "incision in the flesh." It is entered into because of love and devotion. A covenant makes available the power, strength and possessions of each party involved. It links the weaknesses of one to the strengths of the other.

In every time and culture, a blood covenant is the strongest agreement that can be entered into. It carries great spiritual significance.

Even today in a court of law, covenant is the strongest word that can be expressed in the English language to describe an agreement or contract.

Abraham accepted the contract with God. The covenant agreement allowed God to operate in the earth.

Galatians 3:14 says, "That the blessing of Abraham might come on the Gentiles through Jesus Christ; that we might receive the promise of the Spirit through faith." Verse 16 says the promises were made to Abraham and his seed, singular, which is Christ. When Abraham accepted the contract, God was given a way to bring Jesus into the earth. Jesus would be the fulfillment of the Abrahamic covenant. By Abraham's willingness to sacrifice his son, God was able to give His own Son.

Jesus was all man and all God. He was faced with the same temptations as man. He was the exact image of Adam before the Fall. He walked under the Abrahamic covenant with God. He used the word of the written covenant to overcome Satan's temptations. In Matthew 4:4, Jesus said, "It is written, Man shall not live by bread alone, but by every word that proceedeth out of the mouth of God."

Jesus walked perfect and upright under the covenant. God and Jesus were working together. ᴄᴓ

Find Out How the New Covenant in Jesus' Blood Changes Everything for You

FOCUS: "And in like manner, He took the cup after supper, saying, This cup is the new testament or covenant [ratified] in My blood, which is shed (poured out) for you" (Luke 22:20, *The Amplified Bible*).

At the Last Supper, Jesus took His place in the Messiah's chair. He picked up the fourth cup which had previously been left upside down for the Messiah. He told the disciples that this was the cup of the new covenant to be ratified with His blood. He took the center piece of bread, broke it and told them to eat it. He explained to them that this was His body, broken for them. Jesus was foretelling His sufferings. At the Cross He proclaimed, "It is finished."

The Abrahamic covenant had been fulfilled. Jesus became the final sacrifice lifted on the altar of the cross by the high priest. The covenant was ratified by His blood.

> *Because of the new covenant, everything God has belongs to the believer.*

He was in the depths of the earth for three days and nights suffering the penalty of Adam's transgression. When the claims of justice were satisfied, He was raised from the dead. Sin had been paid for.

He took from Satan all the authority he had over the human race. Jesus was born from death to life.

We are born-again, covenant believers. We are redeemed from the curse of the law.

The new covenant has no curse. It is a better covenant, established on better promises. The new covenant is between God and Jesus, a resurrected, untouchable man—it cannot be broken! ൟ

When you make Jesus Lord, your heart is circumcised and you become a covenant man or woman in the Christian covenant.

Now Begin Enjoying It

Galatians 3:29 says if you are Christ's, then you are Abraham's seed and heir according to the promise. That means because of the covenant, everything God has belongs to you as a believer. You can stand on the covenant and exercise what has been promised to you as a believer.

CD 3 Outlined

I. Covenant cut with man
 A. Blood flow
 B. Mutual, binding agreement
 C. Love and devotion
 D. Exchange of authority

II. Jesus under the Abrahamic covenant
 A. Walked perfect before God
 B. Used covenant to overcome Satan
 C. Seed of Abraham (Galatians 3:16)
 D. God's sacrificial Son

III. The blood of Jesus ratified the new covenant
 A. Jesus takes His position as Messiah
   1. Messiah's chair
   2. Fourth cup
   3. Broken bread
 B. Fulfillment of Abrahamic covenant
 C. The new covenant is between God and Jesus
   1. It has no curse
   2. It's unbreakable

IV. When you make Jesus Lord
 A. You become in covenant with God
 B. All God has belongs to you

Study Questions

(1) Why did God have to make a covenant with man? _____

_____

_____

_____

(2) How does a covenant agreement work? _____

_____

_____

_____

(3) How did Jesus fulfill the Abrahamic covenant? _____

_____

_____

_____

_____

(4) Explain the new covenant. _____

_____

_____

_____

(5) What did Jesus mean when He said, "It is finished"? _____

_____

_____

_____

Study Notes

"And if ye be Christ's, then are ye Abraham's seed,
and heirs according to the promise."
Galatians 3:20

4

"Wherefore God also hath highly exalted him, and given him a name which is above every name: That at the name of Jesus every knee should bow, of things in heaven, and things in earth, and things under the earth."

Philippians 2:9-10

God has invested power in the Name of Jesus.

CD FOUR
Reality of the Authority of the Name of Jesus

The Name of Jesus Is Above All Other Names—And God Has Given Us the Right to Use It

What the Name of Jesus Means to You

FOCUS: "And [God] hath put all things under his feet, and gave him to be the head over all things..." (Ephesians 1:22).

God has invested power in the Name of Jesus. You are about to discover how that happened and what it means to the believer today.

The crippled man in Acts 3 was made whole because of the Name of Jesus. Peter said in verse 16 that through faith in the Name of Jesus this man was made strong. Peter and John were just doing what Jesus had commissioned them to do before He was received up into heaven (Mark 16:17).

The authority of the Name of Jesus was even acknowledged by the Sanhedrin. They could not deny that a notable miracle had been done. They commanded Peter and John not to speak in the Name of Jesus:

> Now when they saw the boldness of Peter and John, and...beholding the man which was healed standing with them, they could say nothing against it. But when they had commanded them to go aside out of the council, they conferred among themselves, Saying, What shall we do to these men? for that indeed a notable miracle hath been done by them is manifest to all them that dwell in Jerusalem; and we cannot deny it. But that it spread no further among the people, let us straitly threaten them, that they speak henceforth to no man in this name. And they called them, and commanded them not to speak at all nor teach in the name of Jesus (Acts 4:13-18).

There are three ways in which Jesus obtained the authority and power in His Name. First, Hebrews 1:4 says that *He inherited His Name from God.* To measure the magnitude of this inheritance, the power of God would have to be measured. But God is infinite and His power is immeasurable. The Bible says there is no other name under heaven given among men, whereby we must be saved (Acts 4:12).

Jesus has given full authority in His Name to His Body.

We have the guarantee of a better covenant because His Name is in it, inherited from God. In Hebrews 7:22, Jesus is called the surety of the new covenant. His Name is backing it.

The second way Jesus obtained authority is that *His Name was conferred upon Him.* After Jesus was raised from the dead, He sat down at the right hand of the Father. God spoke to Jesus, a resurrected, reborn man, and called Him God (Hebrews 1:8). God conferred upon Jesus all of the power in this world or any other world.

Philippians 2:9-11 says, "Wherefore God also hath highly exalted him, and given him a name which is above every name: That at the name of Jesus every knee should bow, of things in heaven, and things in earth, and things under the earth; And that every tongue should confess that Jesus Christ is Lord, to the glory of God the Father."

The third and most exciting way Jesus obtained authority in His Name was *by conquest.* In Revelation 1:18 Jesus said, "I am he that liveth, and was dead; and, behold, I am alive for evermore, Amen; and have the keys of hell and of death." Jesus defeated Satan in his own territory (see Colossians 2:15; Hebrews 2:14).

After Jesus paid the price for sin, He exercised His authority and the power of God began to work. The Spirit of God, Who raised Him from the dead, began to strip Satan of all his authority. All the defenses and power Satan had could not match the power of God. Jesus went to Abraham's bosom and preached to the saints there. Satan was no longer in control. ⸎

As a Believer, You Have Power in the Name of Jesus

FOCUS: "…According to the working of his mighty power, Which he wrought in Christ, when he raised him from the dead, and set him at his own right hand in the heavenly places, Far above all principality, and power, and might, and dominion, and every name that is named, not only in this world, but also in that which is to come" (Ephesians 1:19-21).

What is Jesus doing with all this power? He has given full power of attorney to use His name, full authority in His Name to His Body. It belongs to the Body of Christ. Every name that has been named has been put under Jesus' feet, and so it is under the feet of the Body of Christ.

The Name of Jesus is in the earth and it carries authority in three realms. Ephesians 3:15 says, "Of whom the whole family in heaven and earth is named."

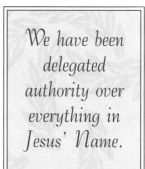

We have been delegated authority over everything in Jesus' Name.

John 16:23 says, "…Whatsoever ye shall ask the Father in my name, he will give it you." We have been given the Name of Jesus and the Word of God to know how to use that Name.

Not only that, the Name of Jesus can do anything He can do because He is backing it. ༁

The Name of Jesus will work if you stand on it and use it. The Holy Spirit will see to it that the Word you speak in faith, in that Name, comes to pass.

Now Begin Enjoying It

The Name of Jesus, used by the believer, is as if Jesus spoke Himself. We have been delegated authority over everything in His Name.

Now learn to exercise dominion with that name!

CD 4 Outlined

I. God invested power in the Name of Jesus

II. Peter used the Name of Jesus—Acts 3:6
   A. Fulfilling the commission—Mark 16:17
   B. Recognized by religious councils as having power

III. How Jesus obtained His authority
   A. Inherited from God—Hebrews 1:4
   B. Conferred upon Him—Philippians 2:9-10
   C. By conquest—Colossians 2:15

IV. The authority in His Name has been given to the Church
   A. A weapon for the Body of Christ
   B. Rights and privileges to use His Name
   C. His Name spoken in faith defeats Satan.

Study Questions

(1) What did Jesus commission His disciples to do? _____

_____

_____

_____

(2) How did Jesus inherit His Name? _____

_____

_____

_____

(3) How was Jesus' Name conferred upon Him? _____

_____

_____

_____

(4) Explain how Jesus obtained His Name through conquest. _____

_____

_____

_____

(5) Why did Jesus give the authority in His Name to the Church? _____

_____

_____

_____

Study Notes

"...In the name of Jesus Christ of Nazareth rise up and walk."
Acts 3:6

"...We pray you in Christ's stead, be ye reconciled to God. For he hath made him to be sin for us, who knew no sin; that we might be made the righteousness of God in him."

2 Corinthians 5:20-21

The born-again believer has been made the righteousness of God in Christ.

CD FIVE
Reality of Righteousness

By Accepting Jesus as His Lord, the Believer No Longer Identifies With Sin but With Righteousness

*T*he born-again believer has been made the righteousness of God. This fact needs to become a reality in his life.

Let Righteousness Become a Reality to You—Live in Victory Here on Earth

FOCUS: "Blessed are they which do hunger and thirst after righteousness: for they shall be filled" (Matthew 5:6).

Righteousness is the greatest blessing of being born again. A man who receives the new birth by faith is no longer a sinner saved by grace. Through Jesus' sacrifice at Calvary, he has been made the righteousness of God. By accepting Jesus as his Lord, he no longer identifies with sin but with righteousness.

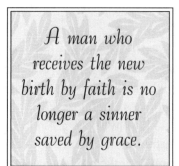

A man who receives the new birth by faith is no longer a sinner saved by grace.

The Greek definition of *righteousness* literally means "being in right-standing." We are in right-standing with God because of what Jesus did. Isaiah 54:17 says, " …their righteousness is of me, saith the Lord." The righteousness of the believer is of God and not of himself. Jesus paid the price at Calvary in order that we might be in right-standing with God.

God's work in Jesus was greater than Satan's work in Adam. The believer receives righteousness because of the price Jesus paid. In the eyes of God, what Jesus did is more powerful than the high treason Adam committed in the Garden.

Hebrews 1:8 says, "But unto the Son he saith, Thy throne, O God, is for ever and ever: a sceptre of righteousness is the sceptre of thy kingdom." When Jesus was raised from the dead, God turned to Him and gave Him the sceptre of righteousness. A sceptre represents an emblem of authority and royalty.

Now Jesus has given us that same right-standing in the family of God.

As a Believer, You Are the Righteousness of God *in Christ*

FOCUS: "For he hath made him to be sin for us, who knew no sin; that we might be made the righteousness of God in him" (2 Corinthians 5:21).

The believer has received the free gift of righteousness. Righteousness is not something obtained by works. It is a gift given at the moment the believer receives Jesus as his Lord (Romans 5:17).

We have been given the Name of Jesus, which assures us entrance into the presence of God. God's ear is attentive to the prayer of the righteous man. James 5:16 says, "The effectual fervent prayer of a righteous man availeth much."

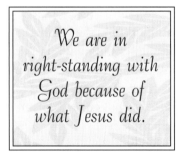

We are in right-standing with God because of what Jesus did.

God has already accepted the sacrifice of Jesus as a substitution for your sin. He has also demanded that you accept that sacrifice for your sin. This sacrifice accepted by man puts God and man back in right relationship. Jesus was made to be sin with man's sinfulness in order for man to be made righteous with His righteousness.

Now God has to treat you as if sin never existed.

Now Begin Enjoying It

Jesus went to the cross and purchased your right to wear the breastplate of righteousness. You are no longer unworthy. You have the ability to stand in the presence of the Father without a sense of guilt, condemnation or inferiority.

Every child of God has exactly the same standing with the Father. You have Jesus' standing with the Father—you are in *right-standing* with God!

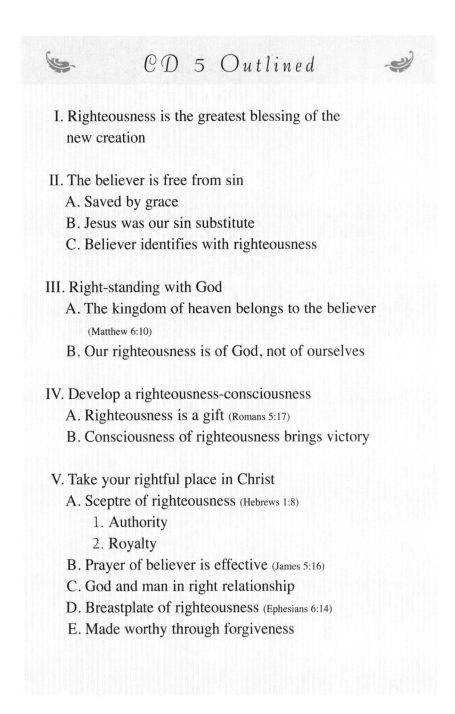

CD 5 Outlined

I. Righteousness is the greatest blessing of the new creation

II. The believer is free from sin
   A. Saved by grace
   B. Jesus was our sin substitute
   C. Believer identifies with righteousness

III. Right-standing with God
   A. The kingdom of heaven belongs to the believer (Matthew 6:10)
   B. Our righteousness is of God, not of ourselves

IV. Develop a righteousness-consciousness
   A. Righteousness is a gift (Romans 5:17)
   B. Consciousness of righteousness brings victory

V. Take your rightful place in Christ
   A. Sceptre of righteousness (Hebrews 1:8)
      1. Authority
      2. Royalty
   B. Prayer of believer is effective (James 5:16)
   C. God and man in right relationship
   D. Breastplate of righteousness (Ephesians 6:14)
   E. Made worthy through forgiveness

Study Questions

(1) Explain why, as a believer, you are not a sinner saved by grace. __

_____

_____

_____

_____

(2) Why does Satan come against those who are in right-standing with God? _____

_____

_____

(3) Why is righteousness a free gift? _____

_____

_____

_____

(4) List some benefits the believer has because of his right-standing.

_____

_____

_____

(5) What does right-standing with God mean to you? _____

_____

_____

_____

Study Notes

"No weapon that is formed against thee shall prosper; and every tongue that shall rise against thee in judgment thou shalt condemn. This is the heritage of the servants of the Lord, and their righteousness is of me, saith the Lord." Isaiah 54:17

6

"*I am crucified with Christ: nevertheless I live; yet not I, but Christ liveth in me: and the life which I now live in the flesh I live by the faith of the Son of God, who loved me, and gave himself for me.*"

Galatians 2:20

Developing a righteousness-consciousness
is renewing the mind to the redemptive work of Christ.

CD SIX

Developing a Righteousness-Consciousness

The Righteousness of God Is for All Believers—There Is No Difference

The believer has been made the righteousness of God *in Christ Jesus*. But in order to take advantage of what that really means, the believer must develop a righteousness-consciousness. Developing a consciousness of right-standing with the Father is the key to living in the fullness of God.

Take Advantage of What Jesus Has Done—Change Your Mind About Yourself

FOCUS: "And be not conformed to this world: but be ye transformed by the renewing of your mind…" (Romans 12:2).

If you have made Jesus Lord of your life, it's time to start seeing yourself in a whole new light. Jesus is in right-standing with God, and those who are in Him have the same standing. Romans 3:25 says that God made Jesus to be "a propitiation through faith in his blood, to declare his righteousness for the remission of sins that are past…." If you are in Christ, your sins are past.

Jesus is the advocate of the Church. The word *advocate* means "lawyer or counselor." Through Jesus, we have legal representation in heaven. The believer can go to Jesus, confess and repent of sin, and he will be cleansed from all unrighteousness (1 John 1:9).

First Corinthians 1:30 says, "But of him are ye in Christ Jesus, who of God is made unto us wisdom, and righteousness, and sanctification, and redemption." That is the truth, but you have to stand for that righteousness and redemption.

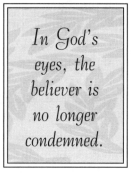

In God's eyes, the believer is no longer condemned.

Stand up to everything Satan tries to bring on you. He has no legal rights over the believer unless granted by the believer himself. Colossians 1:13 says,

"Who hath delivered us from the power of darkness, and hath translated us into the kingdom of his dear Son." You are no longer in Satan's domain of darkness.

When you accept Jesus' sacrifice for your sin, you become the righteousness of God in Christ Jesus.

Righteousness is the ability to stand in the presence of God without a sense of guilt, fear or condemnation, knowing you belong there because of Jesus.

Righteousness is not conduct. Righteousness produces good conduct.

Abraham did not receive the promise because of his works or conduct. His faith in God caused him to receive the promise. Then he walked circumspectly and upright before God.

You see, God deals with individuals according to His Word. You are what God says you are in His Word. When you agree with Him by faith, it's yours.

Jesus received righteousness by faith. Likewise, the believer receives righteousness by receiving Him as Lord in faith. Philippians 3:9 says, "And be found in him, not having mine own righteousness, which is of the law, but that which is through the faith of Christ, the righteousness which is of God by faith." Righteousness is received at salvation. If you can believe you're saved, then you can believe you're the righteousness of God because both are received by faith.

God sees by faith. In God's eyes, the believer is no longer condemned. When he raised Jesus from the dead and broke the bondage of Satan over mankind, the job was completed. The believer was crucified and resurrected from the dead with Jesus, now seated in heavenly places with Him.

Believers can now look at Jesus and see themselves—one with Him, blood-bought children of God, with all the privileges of a king. ༀ

God Sees You in Right-Standing With Jesus

FOCUS: "Therefore if any man be in Christ, he is a new creature: old things are passed away; behold, all things are become new. And all things are of God, who hath reconciled us to himself by Jesus Christ…" (2 Corinthians 5:17-18).

Developing a righteousness-consciousness is renewing the mind to the redemptive work of Christ. In doing so, one will begin to think of who they are in Christ instead of what they were.

First Corinthians 15:34 says, "Awake to righteousness, and sin not…." The believer will reach a place where the mind is renewed to righteousness and a transformation takes place. No longer will righteousness be a question but a reality.

> *Developing a consciousness of right-standing with the Father is the key to living in the fullness of God.*

By meditating on the activities of the flesh, a sin-consciousness will grow. Likewise, by meditating on the things of the spirit, a righteousness-consciousness will develop.

When a person is born again, they are born with all the grace and ability of Jesus. Jesus' earthly ministry is the picture of a believer using the Word and depending on the leadership of the Holy Spirit. He knew He was in right-standing with the Father, therefore, He would not give place to the devil.

By having a righteousness-consciousness, it is just as ridiculous, in the thinking of a believer, for Satan to put sickness on him as it would have been for Satan to put sickness on Jesus.

Now Begin Enjoying It

As a believer, you are in right-standing with God, free from sin and the condemnation of unworthiness. When the believer takes his rightful place in Christ, Satan has no control over any area of his life. So make a decision to see yourself as God sees you—**RIGHTEOUS!**

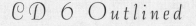

CD 6 Outlined

I. Jesus is our advocate
  A. He represents the believer in heaven
  B. He justifies the believer

II. His righteousness is our righteousness
  A. Philippians 3:9
  B. The believer has no condemnation in God's
     presence
  C. The believer can take his rightful position in Christ

III. Righteousness is by faith
  A. It is not obtained by conduct
  B. It is received at salvation
  C. The believer's faith in Jesus' present position
     1. Jesus' righteousness
     2. 1 Corinthians 1:30

IV. Renew the mind to righteousness
  A. Romans 12:2
  B. The believer identifies with righteousness instead
     of sin
  C. Meditation on righteousness purges
     sin-consciousness

V. Jesus and the believer—identical testimonies
  A. 2 Corinthians 5:15-21
  B. Galatians 2:20
  C. Jesus' earthly ministry—a pattern for the believer

Study Questions

(1) Explain how Jesus is the advocate for the believer. _____

_____

_____

_____

(2) When is the believer made righteous? _____

_____

_____

_____

(3) How do you develop a righteousness-consciousness and a sin-consciousness? _____

_____

_____

_____

(4) What is the difference between a righteousness-consciousness and a sin-consciousness? _____

_____

_____

_____

(5) What does it mean to be righteous or in right-standing with God? ___

_____

_____

_____

Study Notes

"But of Him are ye in Christ Jesus, who of God is made unto us wisdom, and righteousness, and sanctification, and redemption."
1 Corinthians 1:30

"But ye shall receive power, after that the Holy Ghost is come upon you: and ye shall be witnesses unto me both in Jerusalem, and in all Judaea, and in Samaria, and unto the uttermost part of the earth."

Acts 1:8

Jesus has sent the Holy Spirit to live in the believer. He teaches us, guides us and leads us into all truth. With Him dwelling in us, we have the power of God working in our lives.

CD SEVEN
Reality of the Indwelling Holy Spirit I

The Holy Spirit Dwelling in the Believer Empowers Him to Live in Victory

"*A*nd I will pray the Father, and he shall give you another Comforter, that he may abide with you for ever."
John 14:16

The Holy Spirit—Sent to Work in Your Life

FOCUS: "Nevertheless I tell you the truth; It is expedient for you that I go away: for if I go not away, the Comforter will not come unto you; but if I depart, I will send him unto you" (John 16:7).

We see in the Bible that the Holy Spirit is the muscle or power of God. Everywhere the Word is active, the Spirit of God is at work. For instance, Genesis 1:2 says, "… And the Spirit of God moved upon the face of the waters."

The Holy Spirit is the muscle or power of God.

The Spirit of God also *came upon* men of old and moved mightily in their behalf. But now as believers, we can have the Holy Spirit *living in us* and empowering us.

Jesus said it was more profitable for His disciples that He go away, so that He could send the Holy Spirit (John 16:7). The Holy Spirit is our Comforter and Teacher.

In John 14:16, Jesus said, "And I will pray the Father, and he shall give you another Comforter, that he may abide with you for ever." Jesus sent the Holy Spirit to the Church. The Holy Spirit came into His earthly ministry for the benefit of the Body of Christ.

God Has Caused His Spirit to Dwell in You

FOCUS: "...Ye are the temple of the living God; as God hath said, I will dwell in them, and walk in them; and I will be their God, and they shall be my people" (2 Corinthians 6:16).

The believer has become one with God, God working in him to do His good pleasure. Ephesians 3:20 says, "Now unto him that is able to do exceeding abundantly above all that we ask or think, according to the power that worketh in us." That power comes with the indwelling Holy Spirit.

The Holy Spirit did not come to dominate but to comfort, teach, train and counsel the believer. John 16:13 says, "Howbeit when he, the Spirit of truth, is come, he will guide you into all truth: for he shall not speak of himself; but whatsoever he shall hear, that shall he speak: and he will show you things to come."

The Holy Spirit honors the Word of God and causes it to come to pass. Jeremiah 1:12 says God watches over His Word to perform it. The Word will change any situation when it is given absolute authority. The Word is all sovereign and will determine one's success when it is put first place. The Spirit of God will then bring that Word that was acted on in faith to pass.

> *Receiving the Holy Spirit is based on the Word of God, not feelings.*

Spending time in the Word also causes one to become God-inside-minded.

Jesus said in Matthew 8:13, "...as thou hast believed, so be it done unto thee." Feelings do not determine what is received from God.

Receiving the Holy Spirit is based on the Word of God, not feelings. Jesus said that if you ask, you shall receive (Luke 11:11-13).

When a believer receives the infilling of the Holy Spirit, his spirit man has a desire to express himself. Acts 2:4 says, "And they were all filled with the Holy Ghost, and began to speak with other tongues, as the Spirit gave them utterance." The Holy Spirit gives the words but man speaks them. This is the voice of the re-created human spirit expressing himself to God, thereby releasing spiritual power from the inside. A believer who speaks in tongues, speaks unto God and edifies himself (1 Corinthians 14:2, 4). Praying in tongues is the open door to mental and spiritual success.

We receive the Holy Spirit for the same reasons Jesus did. In Luke 4:18-19, Jesus said, "The Spirit of the Lord is upon me, because he hath anointed me to preach the gospel to the poor; he hath sent me to heal the brokenhearted, to preach deliverance to the captives, and recovering of sight to the blind, to set at liberty them that are bruised, To preach the acceptable year of the Lord." ❧

"But ye shall receive power, after that the Holy Ghost is come upon you..." (Acts 1:8).

Now Begin Enjoying It

Jesus told us to go into all the world, lay hands on the sick, cast out devils and speak with new tongues (Mark 16:15-18; John 17:18). He has commissioned us, the Church, to do these things and, with the indwelling Holy Spirit, the very ability of God is in us to do the work.

So take your place, recognize and receive what you can do with the help of the indwelling Holy Spirit. You have the muscle of God ready to work in your life.

CD 7 Outlined

I. The Holy Spirit is the muscle or power of God
  A. He was active from the very beginning (Genesis 1:1-2)
  B. Wherever you see action, you see Him

II. Jesus sent the Holy Spirit
  A. Jesus' personal prayer
  B. Jesus departed; the Holy Spirit arrived
  C. Dwelling place of Holy Spirit
    1. In the Old Testament—He only came *upon* men
    2. In the New Testament—He came to dwell *inside* men (2 Corinthians 6:16)

III. The Holy Spirit reacts to God's Word, bringing it to pass

IV. Become God-inside-minded
  A. Trust the God that is in you
  B. Believe for the things you cannot see
  C. Faith is based on the Word, not feelings
  D. He is in the believer; let Him live through you

V. Spirit of man
  A. Tongues release inner abilities
    1. Speak unto God
    2. For edification
  B. Power came upon you
    1. To be witnesses to all
    2. God's ability in you

Study Questions

(1) Why did Jesus send the Holy Spirit? _____

_____

_____

_____

*(2) What has the Holy Spirit come to do in the life of a believer?*_____

_____

_____

_____

(3) How can one become God-inside-minded? _____

_____

_____

_____

(4) Compare the natural man with the spiritual man. _____

_____

_____

_____

(5) What takes place when the spirit of a believer is expressing himself to God? _____

_____

_____

_____

Study Notes

"...How much more shall your heavenly father
give the Holy Spirit to them that ask him?"
Luke 11:13

"Verily, verily, I say unto you, He that believeth on me, the works that I do shall he do also; and greater works than these shall he do; because I go unto my Father."

John 14:12

The Holy Spirit empowered Jesus to do the works He did. The indwelling Holy Spirit empowers the believer to do the same works, and greater.

CD EIGHT
Reality of the Indwelling Holy Spirit II

"For it is God which worketh
in you both to will and to
do of his good pleasure."
(Philippians 2:13)

We continue in the study of
the Holy Spirit indwelling the
believer. Find out what takes
place in the spirit of a man and
God's purpose of imparting His
power to him.

God Has a Purpose for Filling You With the Holy Spirit

FOCUS: When a born-again man receives the infilling of the Holy Spirit, the Spirit of God is diffused into his spirit, without either losing their identity. Acts 2:4 says, "And they were all filled (diffused throughout their souls) with the Holy Spirit..." (The Amplified Bible).

The Holy Spirit has been sent that God might manifest Himself in the earth. The Holy Spirit undergirds, strengthens, counsels and gives man the ability to fulfill his calling. Ephesians 3:16 says, "That he would grant you, according to the riches of his glory, to be strengthened with might by his Spirit in the inner man."

Jesus was empowered by the Holy Spirit dwelling within Him. When He spoke, power was released. He said, "...The words that I speak unto you I speak not of myself: but the Father that dwelleth in me, he doeth the works" (John 14:10).

In John 14:12, Jesus said, "...He that believeth on me, the works that I do shall he do also." The same works the Father accomplished through Jesus can be done by the believer. It is the power of the Holy Spirit that enables him. The Holy Spirit is the ability of God dwelling inside a man.

When the believer is filled with the Holy Ghost, he is Spirit-filled. He is full of the presence of God. Feelings do not determine the fact of His presence. He has been sent to abide forever (John 14:16).

> *The believer is fully equipped to do the works of God.*

The Holy Spirit Empowers You to Carry Out God's Work in the Earth

FOCUS: "For we are his workmanship, created in Christ Jesus unto good works, which God hath before ordained that we should walk in them" (Ephesians 2:10).

The believer is fully equipped to do the works of God.

In John 14:12, Jesus also said the believer shall do "greater works" than He did. What are the "greater works" that Jesus was referring to?

In Jesus' earthly ministry, He could not get a man born again because Calvary had not taken place. His mission was to set the groundwork so that we could fulfill the Great Commission. He sent the Holy Spirit to enable us to do that.

The day Jesus declared, "It is finished," the Abrahamic covenant was fulfilled. The veil that separated man from the holy of holies was torn from the top down.

No longer would the Holy Spirit dwell in a man-made temple. He would dwell in man and empower him to do the works that God wanted done. The believer is a mobile temple of the living God (see 1 Corinthians 6:19).

> *It is the believer cooperating with the Holy Spirit which enables him to carry out the works.*

By allowing God to work in us, we cannot fail.

Now Begin Enjoying It

God has supplied us with everything necessary to complete the work He has commissioned us to do. Philippians 2:13 says, "For it is God which worketh in you both to will and to do of his good pleasure." Begin to recognize the Holy Spirit dwelling in you, and work together with Him to fulfill your calling.

Remember, you're not alone. Your inner man will be strengthened with might by the Spirit. With His help, you can do the works of Jesus, and even greater works.

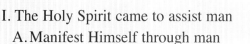

CD 8 Outlined

I. The Holy Spirit came to assist man
  A. Manifest Himself through man
    1. Deliverance for mankind through believer
    2. Guidance for believer

II. Spirit-filled to do good works
  A. God manifested works through Jesus
  B. God manifests works through the believer
    1. Working together with the Holy Spirit
    2. Strengthens inner man
    3. Empowered to do greater works
  C. His presence is not determined by feelings

III. The Holy Spirit no longer dwells in man-made temples
  A. Man is the dwelling place
  B. God lives His life through men
    1. 1 Corinthians 6:19-20
    2. Galatians 2:20

Study Questions

(1) Why does God want His people filled with the Holy Spirit? _____

_____

_____

_____

(2) How does the Holy Spirit help man fulfill his calling? _____

_____

_____

_____

(3) Why was there power in the words of Jesus? _____

_____

_____

_____

(4) How is the believer able to do the works of Jesus? _____

_____

_____

_____

(5) What resulted when the Abrahamic covenant was fulfilled? _____

_____

_____

_____

Study Notes

"For ye are bought with a price: therefore glorify God in your body, and in your spirit, which are God's."
1 Corinthians 6:20

Study Notes

Prayer for Salvation and Baptism
in the Holy Spirit

Heavenly Father, I come to You in the Name of Jesus. Your Word says, "Whosoever shall call on the name of the Lord shall be saved" (Acts 2:21). I am calling on You. I pray and ask Jesus to come into my heart and be Lord over my life according to Romans 10:9-10: "If thou shalt confess with thy mouth the Lord Jesus, and shalt believe in thine heart that God hath raised him from the dead, thou shalt be saved. For with the heart man believeth unto righteousness; and with the mouth confession is made unto salvation." I do that now. I confess that Jesus is Lord, and I believe in my heart that God raised Him from the dead.

I am now reborn! I am a Christian—a child of Almighty God! I am saved! You also said in Your Word, "If ye then, being evil, know how to give good gifts unto your children: HOW MUCH MORE shall your heavenly Father give the Holy Spirit to them that ask him?" (Luke 11:13). I'm also asking You to fill me with the Holy Spirit. Holy Spirit, rise up within me as I praise God. I fully expect to speak with other tongues as You give me the utterance (Acts 2:4). In Jesus' Name. Amen!

Begin to praise God for filling you with the Holy Spirit. Speak those words and syllables you receive—not in your own language, but the language given to you by the Holy Spirit. You have to use your own voice. God will not force you to speak. Don't be concerned with how it sounds. It is a heavenly language!

Continue with the blessing God has given you and pray in the spirit every day.

You are a born-again, Spirit-filled believer. You'll never be the same!

Find a good church that boldly preaches God's Word and obeys it. Become part of a church family who will love and care for you as you love and care for them.

We need to be connected to each other. It increases our strength in God. It's God's plan for us.

Make it a habit to watch the *Believer's Voice of Victory* television broadcast and become a doer of the Word, who is blessed in his doing (James 1:22-25).

About the Author

Kenneth Copeland is co-founder and president of Kenneth Copeland Ministries in Fort Worth, Texas, and best-selling author of books that include *How to Discipline Your Flesh* and *Honor—Walking in Honesty, Truth and Integrity*.

Since 1967, Kenneth has been a minister of the gospel of Christ and teacher of God's Word. He is also the artist on award-winning albums such as his Grammy-nominated *Only the Redeemed, In His Presence, He Is Jehovah, Just a Closer Walk* and his most recently released *Big Band Gospel* album. He also co-stars as the character Wichita Slim in the children's adventure videos *The Gunslinger, Covenant Rider* and the movie *The Treasure of Eagle Mountain,* and as Daniel Lyon in the Commander Kellie and the Superkids™ videos *Armor of Light* and *Judgment: The Trial of Commander Kellie.* Kenneth also co-stars as a Hispanic godfather in the 2009 movie *The Rally.*

With the help of offices and staff in the United States, Canada, England, Australia, South Africa, Ukraine and Singapore, Kenneth is fulfilling his vision to boldly preach the uncompromised Word of God from the top of this world, to the bottom, and all the way around. His ministry reaches millions of people worldwide through daily and Sunday TV broadcasts, magazines, teaching audios and videos, conventions and campaigns, and the World Wide Web.

When The LORD first spoke to Kenneth and Gloria Copeland about starting the *Believer's Voice of Victory* magazine...

He said: *This is your seed. Give it to everyone who ever responds to your ministry, and don't ever allow anyone to pay for a subscription!*

For more than 40 years, it has been the joy of Kenneth Copeland Ministries to bring the good news to believers. Readers enjoy teaching from ministers who write from lives of living contact with God, and testimonies from believers experiencing victory through God's WORD in their everyday lives.

Today, the *BVOV* magazine is mailed monthly, bringing encouragement and blessing to believers around the world. Many even use it as a ministry tool, passing it on to others who desire to know Jesus and grow in their faith!

Request your FREE subscription to the *Believer's Voice of Victory* magazine today!

Go to **freevictory.com** to subscribe online, or call us at **1-800-600-7395** (U.S. only) or **+1-817-852-6000**.

We're Here for You!®

Your growth in God's WORD and victory in Jesus are at the very center of our hearts. In every way God has equipped us, we will help you deal with the issues facing you, so you can be the **victorious overcomer** He has planned for you to be.

The mission of Kenneth Copeland Ministries is about all of us growing and going together. Our prayer is that you will take full advantage of all The LORD has given us to share with you.

Wherever you are in the world, you can watch the *Believer's Voice of Victory* broadcast on television (check your local listings), the Internet at kcm.org or on our digital Roku channel.

Our website, **kcm.org,** gives you access to every resource we've developed for your victory. And, you can find contact information for our international offices in Africa, Asia, Australia, Canada, Europe, Ukraine and our headquarters in the United States.

Each office is staffed with devoted men and women, ready to serve and pray with you. You can contact the worldwide office nearest you for assistance, and you can call us for prayer at our U.S. number, +1-817-852-6000, 24 hours every day!

We encourage you to connect with us often and let us be part of your everyday walk of faith!

Jesus Is LORD!

Kenneth & Gloria Copeland

Kenneth and Gloria Copeland